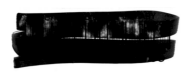

D1606661

SCIENCE vs. DISEASE

by Nick Hunter

Gareth Stevens
Publishing

Please visit our website, www.garethstevens.com. For a free color catalog of all our high-quality books, call toll free 1-800-542-2595 or fax 1-877-542-2596.

Library of Congress Cataloging-in-Publication Data

Anniss, Matt.
 Science vs. disease / Matt Anniss.
    pages ; cm. — (Science fights back)
 Title from table of contents: Science vs. disease
 Includes index.
 ISBN 978-1-4339-8688-8 (pbk.)
 ISBN 978-1-4339-8689-5 (6-pack)
 ISBN 978-1-4339-8687-1 (library binding)
 1. Medical sciences—History. 2. Science—History. 3. Medicine—History. I. Title. II. Title: Science vs. disease. III. Title: Science versus disease.
 R133.A595 2013
 610.9—dc23

                                        2012034538
First Edition

Published in 2013 by
Gareth Stevens Publishing
111 East 14th Street, Suite 349
New York, NY 10003

Produced by Calcium, www.calciumcreative.co.uk
Designed by Simon Borrough
Edited by Sarah Eason and Harriet McGregor

Photo credits: Dreamstime: Aragorn1785 22, Marilyn Barbone 32, Dreamshot 14, Glazyuk cover br, Godfer 40, Monkey Business Images 23, Davide Romanini 20t, David Snyder 9, Weixin Shen 3, 15, Williamju 33; Shutterstock: Africa924 4, AISPIX by Image Source 21, Ryan Rodrick Beiler 20b, BestPhotoStudio 43, Brian Chase 34, Stephen Coburn 28, Matthew Cole 30, Dundanim 16, Lisa Eastman 26, Fotana 7, Markus Gann 29, Illusionstudio 41, Sebastian Kaulitzki 12, 36, Levent Konuk 19, Henrik Larsson 8, Mikeledray 18, Monkey Business Images 37, Tyler Olson 35, Picsfive 17, 25, Paul Prescott 11, SandiMako 5, Dmitriy Shironosov 10, Stefanolunardi 38, Swissmacky 6, James Thew cover tl, 13, Tungphoto 42, Valentina R. 27, Wavebreakmedia ltd 24, Andrey Yurlov 31, ZF 39.

Printed in the United States of America

CPSIA compliance information: Batch #CW13GS: For further information contact Gareth Stevens, New York, New York at 1-800-542-2595.

Contents

Life and Death

The battle against disease is one that the human race has faced for many thousands of years. In the past, it was one that we were destined to lose. Today, there are far fewer illnesses for which there is no cure. We owe this huge transformation in our lives to science.

RAPID IMPROVEMENTS

Over the last 100 years, scientific discoveries have helped us to understand the human body better than ever before. We've found cures for many dangerous diseases and have wiped out deadly infections. We've invented machines that do the work of the heart and lungs, and discovered the tiny, microscopic parts that are the very basis of life itself.

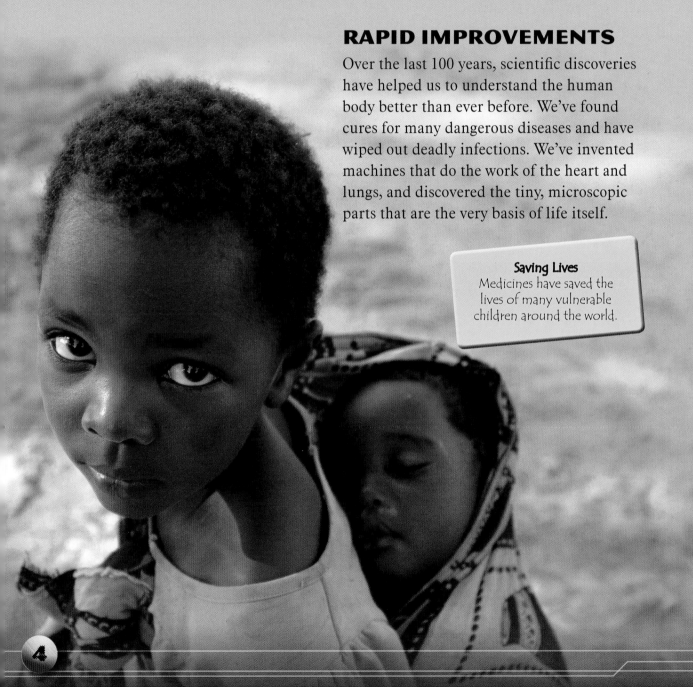

Saving Lives
Medicines have saved the lives of many vulnerable children around the world.

FIGHTING DISEASE

In laboratories all over the world, scientists have found ways to make medicines that help our bodies to fight diseases. Other scientists have invented machines that can fix our eyesight using lasers. Today, heart attack victims can be brought back to life, and life-saving surgery is performed using tiny cameras the size of a pinhead.

AMAZING JOURNEY

Science's battle against disease can mean the difference between life and death, and between agonizing suffering and blissful pain relief. Our scientific discoveries can help people to walk, see, and hear again.

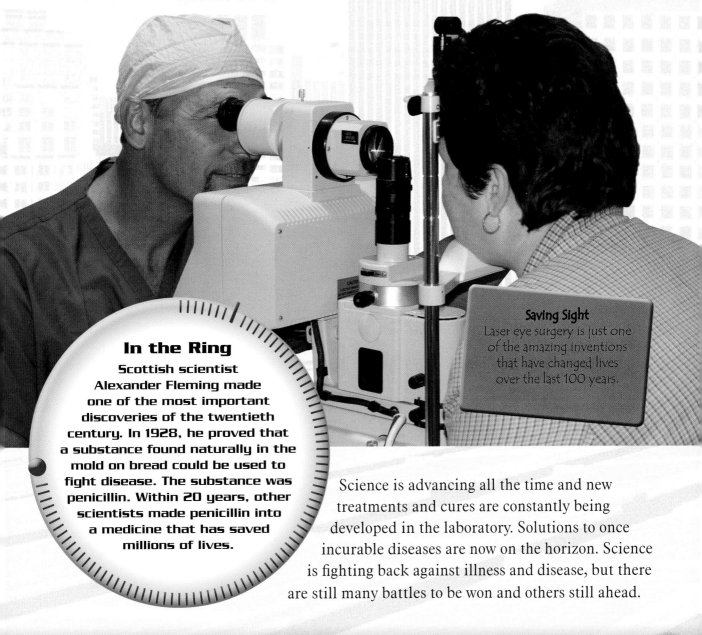

In the Ring

Scottish scientist Alexander Fleming made one of the most important discoveries of the twentieth century. In 1928, he proved that a substance found naturally in the mold on bread could be used to fight disease. The substance was penicillin. Within 20 years, other scientists made penicillin into a medicine that has saved millions of lives.

Saving Sight
Laser eye surgery is just one of the amazing inventions that have changed lives over the last 100 years.

Science is advancing all the time and new treatments and cures are constantly being developed in the laboratory. Solutions to once incurable diseases are now on the horizon. Science is fighting back against illness and disease, but there are still many battles to be won and others still ahead.

Chapter One: Killer Epidemics

There are few things that scientists fear more than a deadly epidemic. An epidemic is when an infectious disease—one that can be passed from person to person, such as measles or flu—spreads rapidly, often over a large area. Within days, a whole town can be infected. Within weeks, the disease can spread to other towns, cities, or even countries.

WORLDWIDE REACH

When an epidemic, also called a "disease outbreak," begins to spread around the world, it becomes known as a "pandemic." When an epidemic becomes a pandemic, it could kill hundreds, thousands, or even millions of people.

Pandemic Fear
Many people in Asia wore masks to try to avoid catching bird flu when there was fear of a pandemic spread in 2004–2005.

THE PLAGUE

Over the course of human history, many millions of people have died because of epidemics and pandemics. In the Middle Ages, a disease known as "the plague" or "black death" killed more than 75 million people in Europe, including more than half of the population of England. Another disease called smallpox killed hundreds of millions of people over two centuries.

The Age of Protection
Vaccines, here packed and ready to be shipped to hospitals, now help to protect us against epidemics.

CONSTANT BATTLE

Scientists are always fighting a battle to prevent another global pandemic. They do this through research into infectious diseases and also by developing vaccines. Vaccines are medicines that help people to build up a natural resistance to diseases.

In countries such as the United States, vaccine injections are often given to children to protect against measles and other infectious diseases. Once a person has been given this injection, they will be protected against the disease if they ever come into contact with it.

Winning or Losing?

Scientists have wiped out certain epidemics and pandemics. Yet the battle is still not yet won. Within our lifetime, it is likely that deadly new strains of diseases will develop and threaten the lives of many people worldwide.

Disease in the Developing World

In recent times, very few epidemics and pandemics have affected people in more developed countries, where medicine is highly advanced and readily available. However, epidemics are still killing many millions around the world, particularly in developing places in Africa and Asia where there is little health care.

POVERTY CURSE

Deadly diseases are most likely to do the greatest amount of harm in countries where poverty is widespread. This is because low-quality living conditions and a lack of fresh water make the spread of infectious diseases more likely.

TROPICAL PANDEMIC

Currently the two most dangerous pandemics are malaria and HIV/AIDS. Malaria is a tropical disease caused by a virus that affects up to 350 million people every year. A virus is a tiny infectious agent. Mosquitoes usually pass the virus from person to person. It is not necessarily deadly and can easily be treated by medicines, but many people in poor parts of Africa, South America, and Asia do not have access to these treatments.

Dying from Malaria
Many people in Africa still die every year after being bitten by a mosquito carrying malaria.

NO KNOWN CURE

More alarming is the continued rise in cases of HIV/AIDS because a cure has not yet been found. AIDS is a highly infectious disease caused by the HIV virus, which is transmitted from person to person by intimate sexual contact. In parts of Africa, it is estimated that more than 25 percent of the population is infected with the HIV virus. These people are described as "HIV positive."

NEW DRUGS

HIV/AIDS weakens the body's natural defenses against illness. Scientists have developed drugs to treat the symptoms and prolong the life of sufferers. With many millions dying around the world each year, the pressure is on for scientists to find a solution.

Living with AIDS
These children in Ghana, Africa, are raising awareness of the devastating effects of HIV/AIDS in their communities.

Breaking Through

In 2007 in Germany, an HIV-positive man named Timothy Ray Brown was given a bone marrow transplant to try to cure his leukemia. The bone marrow came from people whose white blood cells were resistant to the HIV virus. The treatment targeted both diseases, providing hope that other HIV-positive patients could be treated in the future a similar way.

Success Stories

The battle against disease has been raging for a long time. Over the years, doctors and scientists have been able to control the spread of diseases, thanks to the development of vaccines.

KILLER SMALLPOX

The development of one vaccine helped doctors wipe out one of the most deadly diseases in history—smallpox. During the eighteenth and nineteenth centuries, smallpox was common throughout the world and killed an estimated 400,000 Europeans every year. The development of the smallpox vaccine by Edward Jenner in 1796 changed this terrifying statistic. By the start of the twentieth century, smallpox deaths in the United States and Europe had dropped dramatically, thanks to smallpox vaccine injections.

The last confirmed death from smallpox occurred in Birmingham, England, in 1978. A year later, the World Health Organization (WHO) finally announced that smallpox had been wiped out worldwide.

Searching for Answers
Scientists can spend years studying deadly diseases in laboratories in the hope that they will find a cure.

DEADLY POLIO

Since 1988, the WHO and the charity UNICEF have been determined to destroy another disease that has killed or paralyzed millions in the developing world. This deadly and crippling disease is polio.

Vaccines to protect against polio infection were developed by scientists in the 1950s. Widespread use of the vaccine meant that by the 1970s, very few cases were reported in developed countries. Yet epidemics continue to be reported to this day in Africa and Asia.

Since 1988, infection rates worldwide have fallen from 400,000 a year to less than 1,000. The disease now only exists as an epidemic in three countries—Pakistan, Afghanistan, and Nigeria. It is hoped that within the next 10 years the disease will be wiped out completely.

In the Ring

In 1957, an American scientist named Albert Sabin announced that he had developed a cheap, effective polio vaccine. Sabin's vaccine was not injected into the body, but given in the mouth as a few drops of liquid. Sabin's vaccine has since saved the lives of many millions of children worldwide.

Victims of Polio
Polio can cripple its victims, leaving sufferers unable to walk without the aid of crutches.

Disease Fights Back

We like to think of most viruses as relatively harmless—things that we pick up from coming into contact with sick people or not washing our hands. Yet infectious diseases are caused by viruses, tiny particles that can do great harm. Like animals, viruses are continually adapting to their environment in order to survive.

MUTATIONS

Because scientists have developed vaccines to protect against many common diseases, these diseases are beginning to adapt— or "mutate"—to protect themselves. If a disease enters the body of someone who is protected against it, it will come up against stiff resistance and ultimately die. These diseases need our bodies to survive, so they must mutate constantly.

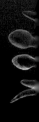

Changing to Survive
This image shows a virus as seen with the aid of a microscope. Viruses change their form to survive.

RESISTING TREATMENT

Disease "adaptation" is happening all the time. Scientists are already reporting that certain viruses, including the malaria virus, have built up a resistance to the vaccines. When this happens, scientists need to develop new cures. As viruses are constantly mutating, scientists across the world are continually fighting a battle to stay one step ahead of nature.

One virus that has shown great "adaptability" is influenza, commonly known as "flu." There are many different versions of the flu virus. On the whole, they are not deadly and there are vaccines to protect against them. However, in recent years, some new strains of flu have been discovered.

Breaking Through

In 2011, scientists in California announced that they believed a "universal flu vaccine"— one that would protect against all strains of the virus—could be developed within two years. This would offer protection for up to 10 years. Current vaccines usually protect against a single strain for around one year, by which time the virus will have mutated once more.

Searching for Signs
Scientists study viruses carefully and look for any signs of new mutations that could trigger an epidemic.

Fighting Flu

Influenza, or flu, is one of the most difficult diseases to control. It mutates to avoid destruction by scientists. Different strains of flu are also found in birds and animals. There is always the possibility that these strains will mutate into viruses than can kill humans.

BIRD FLU OUTBREAK

In 2003, four people in Asia died from a type of flu passed on by chickens. Scientists quickly identified it as a new strain of avian flu, also known as bird flu. Luckily, bird flu didn't spread too quickly, and only 330 people have died worldwide from the disease. However, the threat to human life was enough to persuade the United States government and drug companies to invest billions of dollars in developing a vaccine.

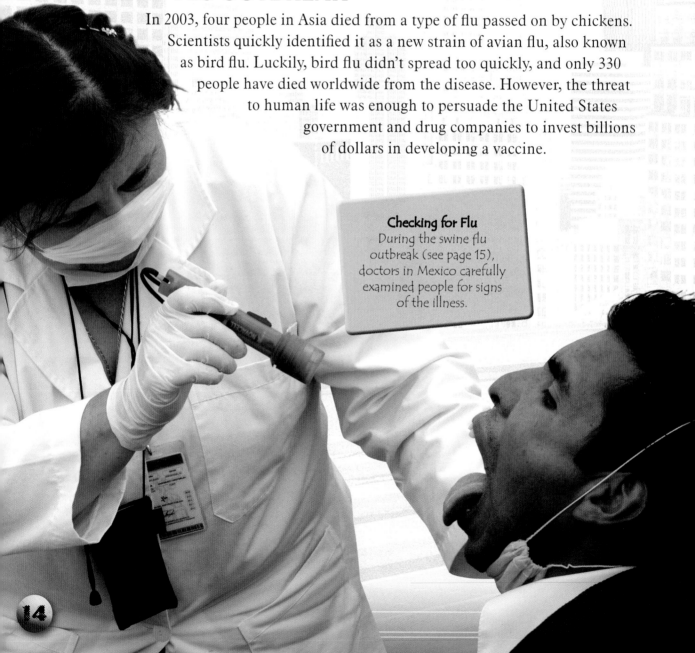

Checking for Flu
During the swine flu outbreak (see page 15), doctors in Mexico carefully examined people for signs of the illness.

Controlling Epidemics
When swine flu spread worldwide in 2009, Chinese officials screened travelers for signs of the disease.

Winning or Losing?

Billions of dollars are spent each year on scientific research into treatments for influenza. More successful vaccines are being developed all the time. Yet the flu virus mutates so fast that experts fear that we will never truly win the battle. It is always possible that a new strain could develop and kill millions before scientists find a cure.

FROM PIGS TO HUMANS

In 2009, another new strain of flu rapidly spread worldwide and became a pandemic. This particular strain was known as "swine flu," as it was first discovered in Mexican pig farmers. When scientists researched the virus, they found that it was similar to strains previously found in pigs, birds, and humans.

When the first confirmed cases of what scientists called "H1N1/09" swine flu were discovered in March 2009, the WHO sent out a warning of a possible global pandemic. Within weeks, the virus had spread to all parts of the world.

It wasn't long before drug companies had developed a vaccine to protect against the virus. Governments across the world ordered billions of dollars worth of vaccines to protect children, old people, and pregnant women. Thankfully, a crisis was averted.

Chapter Two: Changing and Saving Lives

One hundred years ago, men and women in the United States rarely lived beyond the age of 50. Now, average life expectancy is almost 80 years. In another century, people will expect to live until they are 100 years old.

CENTURY OF CHANGE

We have science to thank for the fact that we all live longer today. Around 100 years ago, relatively minor infections could become life threatening, and most heart attacks nearly always resulted in death. People also lived under the threat of picking up horrible diseases such as smallpox and polio, which scarred them for life.

Living for Longer
Today, modern medicine helps many people live well into old age.

SCIENTIFIC WONDERS

Thanks to the wonders of modern science, we can now transplant organs such as the heart, lungs, or kidneys from one person to another. We can use small doses of radiation to cure cancer. We create artificial legs to help wounded soldiers to walk again, and even use cosmetic surgery to repair damaged body parts when people are hurt in fires or accidents.

STAYING ALIVE

Scientists have also developed machines that can perform the functions of human organs. Life support machines can keep people alive by breathing for them. Dialysis machines clean and filter the blood when kidneys fail. Pacemakers help the heart to pump blood around the body and incubators help tiny babies to stay alive.

Science has helped to prolong life and cure previously incurable diseases. Every day, the work of scientists around the world is helping to change and save lives everywhere.

Breaking Through

In 2012, scientists in Israel created new "beating" heart cells in a laboratory. They did this using skin cells from heart-attack patients. In the future, they hope to use the same technique to repair damaged hearts and help people live longer.

Setting the Pace
Pacemakers are tiny devices that are inserted into the human heart to make it beat at a regular pace.

Transplants

Disease can damage the body and destroy vital organs. In the past, those suffering from kidney disease, heart problems, or lung disease had little or no chance of survival. Now, thanks to organ transplant surgery, they have every chance of enjoying a longer and healthier life.

COMPLEX PROCESS

Transplant surgery is the process of taking a body part from one person and putting it into the body of another. Transplant donors can be either alive or dead, depending on the body part being donated. The donor or the donor's family must also agree to the process and be fully aware of the risks of any operation involved.

Doctors usually see transplant surgery as a last resort. Finding donors willing to give up vital organs isn't easy. Sadly, there is always a risk that the patient's body will reject the replacement organ or body part.

Breaking Through

In March 2012, surgeons in Maryland performed the most intensive transplant to date. Over 36 hours, they successfully managed to transplant a donor's entire face—including cheekbones, jaw, eyelids, skin, nose, and teeth—onto a man who had been injured in a gun accident.

Replacing Hearts
Around 2,300 heart transplant operations are carried out in the United States every year.

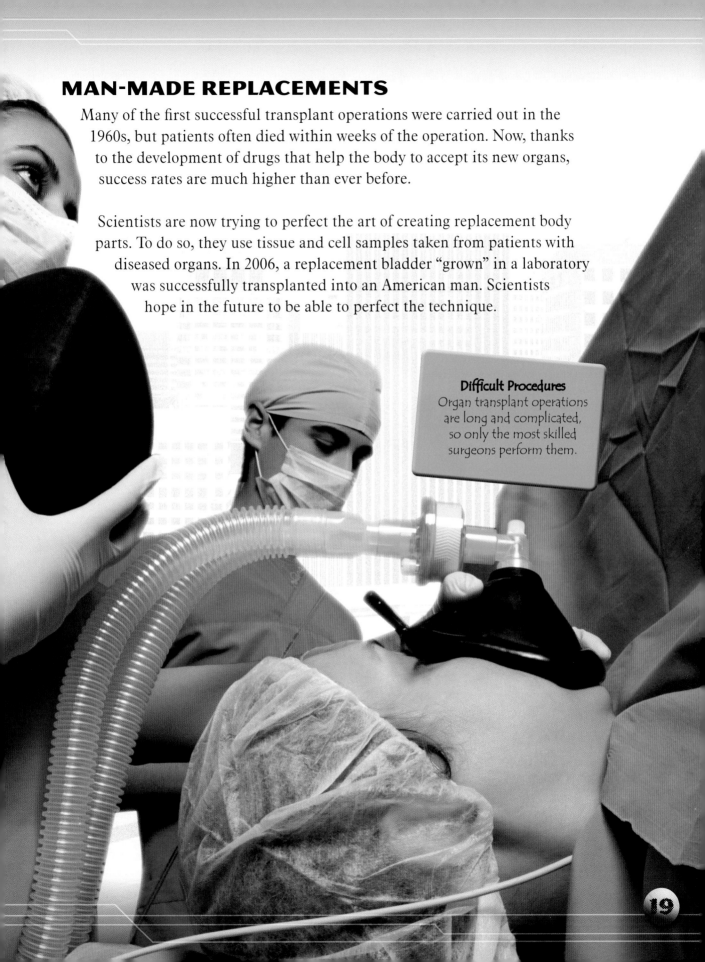

MAN-MADE REPLACEMENTS

Many of the first successful transplant operations were carried out in the 1960s, but patients often died within weeks of the operation. Now, thanks to the development of drugs that help the body to accept its new organs, success rates are much higher than ever before.

Scientists are now trying to perfect the art of creating replacement body parts. To do so, they use tissue and cell samples taken from patients with diseased organs. In 2006, a replacement bladder "grown" in a laboratory was successfully transplanted into an American man. Scientists hope in the future to be able to perfect the technique.

Difficult Procedures
Organ transplant operations are long and complicated, so only the most skilled surgeons perform them.

Artificial Limbs

In recent years, scientists have made a number of great advances in the field of prosthetics. This is the science of creating artificial arms, legs, hands, and other external body parts. These body parts replace those lost or injured in accidents.

Athletes and Artificial Limbs
Artificial limbs allow disabled athletes to compete at the highest level.

ALMOST REAL

Now, it is possible for scientists to make prosthetic limbs that work in similar ways to real limbs. They use metal, plastic, and robot electronics to make new arms, legs, and hands. The body parts are capable of lifting objects, turning door handles, and, most amazingly, even being controlled by thought.

Perfect Fit
These artificial limbs were made exactly the right size for a young Lebanese boy injured by bombing.

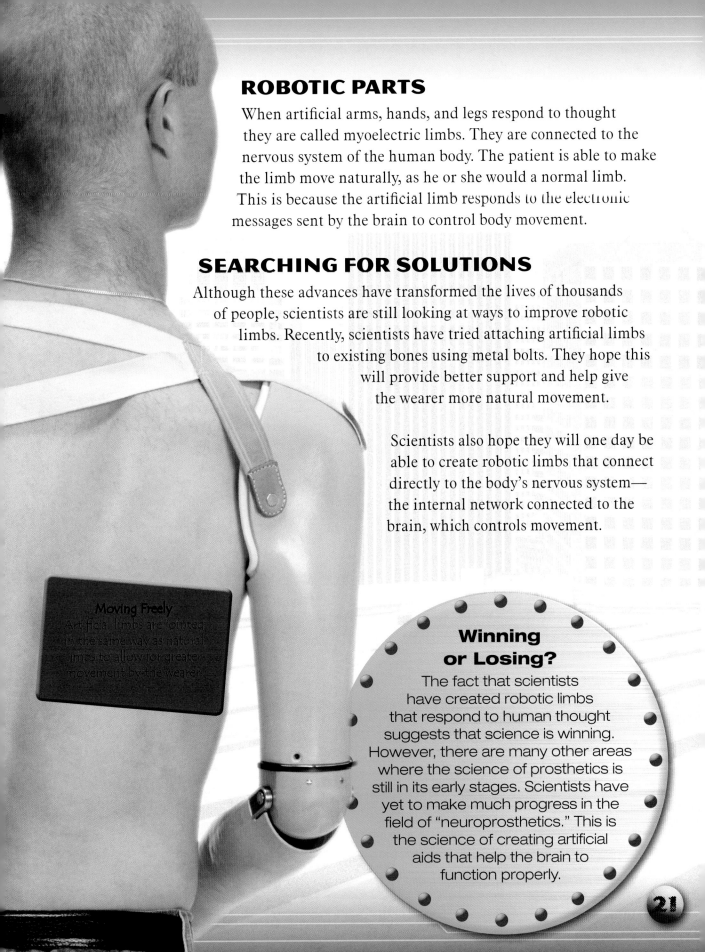

ROBOTIC PARTS

When artificial arms, hands, and legs respond to thought they are called myoelectric limbs. They are connected to the nervous system of the human body. The patient is able to make the limb move naturally, as he or she would a normal limb. This is because the artificial limb responds to the electronic messages sent by the brain to control body movement.

SEARCHING FOR SOLUTIONS

Although these advances have transformed the lives of thousands of people, scientists are still looking at ways to improve robotic limbs. Recently, scientists have tried attaching artificial limbs to existing bones using metal bolts. They hope this will provide better support and help give the wearer more natural movement.

Scientists also hope they will one day be able to create robotic limbs that connect directly to the body's nervous system— the internal network connected to the brain, which controls movement.

Moving Freely
Artificial limbs are jointed in the same way as natural limbs to allow for greater movement by the wearer.

Winning or Losing?

The fact that scientists have created robotic limbs that respond to human thought suggests that science is winning. However, there are many other areas where the science of prosthetics is still in its early stages. Scientists have yet to make much progress in the field of "neuroprosthetics." This is the science of creating artificial aids that help the brain to function properly.

Surgical Cures

Most operations are performed by surgeons cutting into the body and opening it up. This allows them to fix diseased organs, ruptured blood vessels, and injured body parts using conventional surgery. Surgeons are skilled and rarely make mistakes. However, any surgical operation involves risks—one error, and a patient could be battling for their life.

KEYHOLE SURGERY

In recent years, scientists have helped develop techniques that make performing operations a great deal safer. One such technique is keyhole surgery. This type of surgery got its name due to the tiny incisions made to perform keyhole operations.

During surgery, a small cut is made in the body, into which a thin cable is inserted. On the end of the cable is a minute camera. This allows the surgeon to get a close-up view of inside the patient's body. The surgeon can then carry out the operation using minute, specially adapted instruments, which are controlled electronically. Keyhole surgery makes operations much quicker and also speeds up the patient's recovery time after surgery.

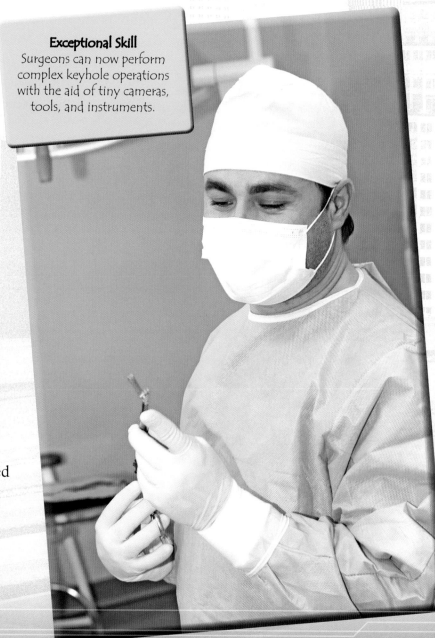

Exceptional Skill
Surgeons can now perform complex keyhole operations with the aid of tiny cameras, tools, and instruments.

LASER SURGERY

Another new technique that has proved popular in recent years is laser surgery to correct vision. This uses thin laser beams to re-shape the front of the eye in order to improve sight. The lasers are controlled by a computer, and can therefore make very accurate cuts into the eye to repair damage.

Laser eye surgery is very popular, but it is not without risks. Some people report bad side-effects after the operation, such as seeing double, dizziness, and, although very rare, even the loss of their sight.

In the Ring

Although keyhole surgery wasn't common until the late twentieth century, the first ever keyhole procedure was actually carried out in 1910 by a Swedish surgeon called Hans Christian Jacobaeus. He had no tiny video camera to help him, but he did develop his own microscopic instruments.

Seeing Again

Every year, hundreds of thousands of people regain their sight after receiving laser eye surgery.

Supporting the Body

Around the world, many lives are saved thanks to machines invented by scientists to do the jobs of our body organs. Very sick people can sometimes be kept alive for weeks, months, or even years, thanks to these incredible inventions.

LIFE SUPPORT

Perhaps the most amazing machine invented in the last 60 years is the heart-lung machine, often called a "life support machine." This device is often used by doctors in intensive care or during heart surgery. It performs the tasks usually done by the heart and lungs. Not only does it pump blood around the body—the job of the heart—but it also makes sure that there is enough oxygen in the blood for the patient to survive until they have recovered.

Defibrillator machines can restart the heart by sending an electric shock through the body that triggers the heart muscle. Mechanical ventilation machines can replace regular breathing. They pump air in and out of lungs if they're not working.

Saving Lives
Doctors can now use defibrillators to save patients who would once have died without these machines.

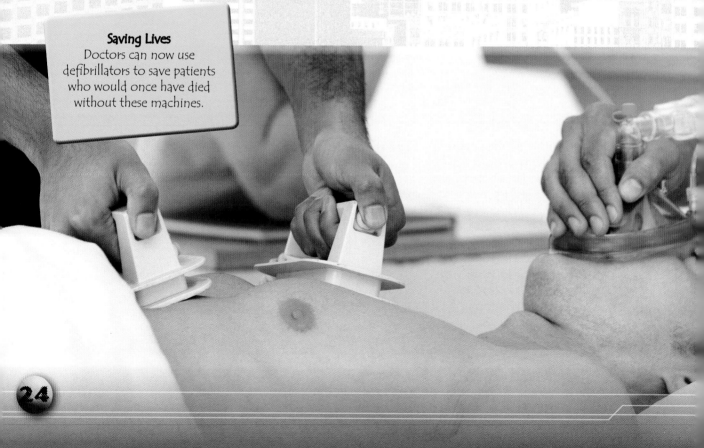

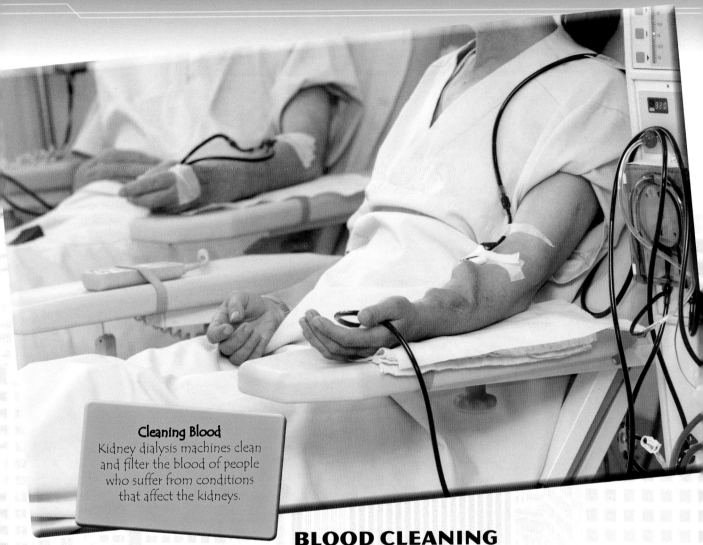

Cleaning Blood
Kidney dialysis machines clean and filter the blood of people who suffer from conditions that affect the kidneys.

In the Ring

The first mechanical heart machine was built by Detroit heart surgeon Dr. Forest Dewey Dodrill and car manufacturer General Motors. Called the Dodrill-GMR, it was first used during a heart operation in July 1953. The operation was a huge success and Dodrill's machine became the blueprint for heart-lung machines.

BLOOD CLEANING

Another incredible invention that has saved many lives is the kidney dialysis machine. The kidneys are vital to our survival because they clean our blood, filtering out all of the waste. If the kidneys fail, no clean blood will circulate round the body and a person will eventually die of severe blood poisoning.

Many patients with kidney failure have been kept alive because of dialysis machines. These devices remove blood from the body, clean it, and then pump it back in. Many patients with kidneys that don't work have been able to live longer and healthier lives because they receive regular dialysis sessions to clean their blood.

Against the Odds

In the past, it was not uncommon for newborn babies to die within hours or days of birth. Now, thanks to the work of scientists, even babies born prematurely, before they have had time to fully develop, have a great chance of survival.

Doctors now have the technology to monitor the progress of a baby before birth using a machine called a sonograph. Based on the same radar technology used to keep track of flying airplanes, the device allows doctors to listen to the unborn baby's heartbeat.

Modern Care
All babies are carefully checked after birth and during the first weeks of their lives to make sure they are healthy.

SPECIAL CARE

Saving the lives of premature, weak, or sick babies requires a lot of specialist care. There are now many hospitals that have specialist neonatal intensive care units that are equipped to care for very weak and sick newborn babies.

These units have special machines called incubators, in which premature babies sleep. Incubators keep the babies warm, protect them from infection, and help them breathe. Modern incubators also monitor the baby's temperature and heartbeat. These incubators have saved the lives of countless tiny babies.

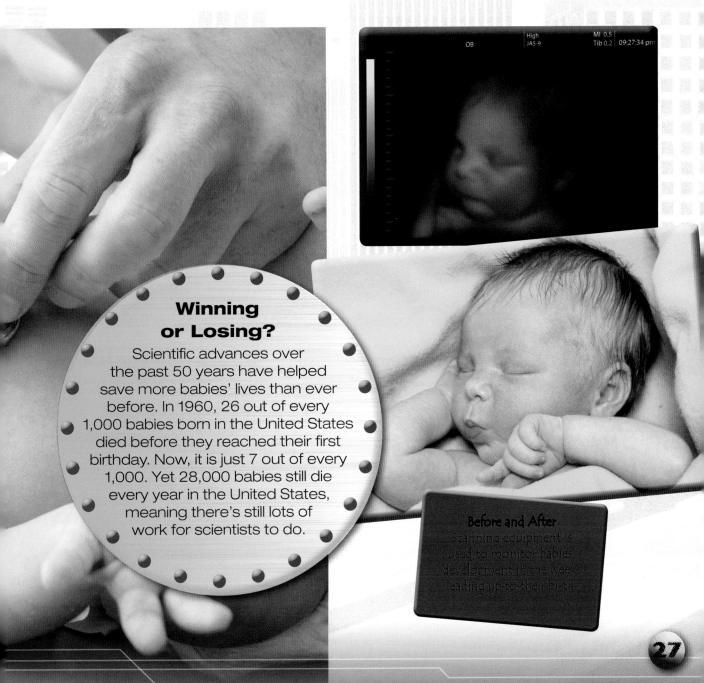

Winning or Losing?

Scientific advances over the past 50 years have helped save more babies' lives than ever before. In 1960, 26 out of every 1,000 babies born in the United States died before they reached their first birthday. Now, it is just 7 out of every 1,000. Yet 28,000 babies still die every year in the United States, meaning there's still lots of work for scientists to do.

Before and After
Scanning equipment is used to monitor babies' development in the weeks leading up to their birth.

27

Chapter Three: The Human Body

The human body is an incredibly complex machine capable of great achievements, be it running 100 meters in under 10 seconds, figuring out the mysteries of the universe, or even learning to walk and talk. Yet, we still know very little about our bodies.

Under the Microscope
The invention of powerful microscopes is allowing scientists to investigate the tiniest parts of our bodies.

ELECTRON MICROSCOPE

The study of the human body is not a new science—people have been studying it for well over 500 years. Yet it's only in the last two centuries that equipment has existed to allow us to accurately investigate our incredible bodies.

AMAZING DEVICE

We now know more about the human body than ever before, and it's thanks largely to the development of the electron microscope. Scientists have been using regular light microscopes to enlarge images of very tiny objects since the seventeenth century. But the electron microscope is different. The device allows scientists to look at objects that are 10 million times too small for the naked eye to see.

In the Ring

Accurate plans for the first ever electron microscope were drawn up by a Hungarian scientist named Leo Szilar in 1931. He didn't want to build the microscope, however, and left the task to German engineers Ernst Ruska and Max Knoll.

SCIENTIFIC REVOLUTION

The electron microscope started a revolution. It meant that scientists could see the tiny particles that form the very building blocks of everything on Earth. They could also look closely at every part of our body, inside and out, to discover how it worked. All the drugs we take to cure illnesses, the vaccines that protect us, and the surgical procedures doctors perform on us would not be possible without the invention of the electron microscope.

Today's microscopes are millions of times more powerful than the first electron microscope. These machines allow scientists to find out awesome facts about our bodies all the time.

Tiniest Parts
This is what a cell looks like under a microscope. We have trillions of cells in our bodies.

Mapping the Human Genome

In the year 2000, President Bill Clinton and British Prime Minister Tony Blair announced one of the greatest scientific achievements of all time—the mapping of the human genome. It had taken 30 years of research and cost more than $3 billion, but it was a revolutionary discovery. Now scientists knew exactly how the very tiniest elements of the human body fit together.

DNA Magic
Each colored bar of this DNA image represents an individual gene.

In the Ring

Although scientists had an idea that human DNA existed as far back as the 1890s, it wasn't until 1953 that it was confirmed and accurately mapped out. That discovery was the work of two pioneering scientists, an American called James D. Watson and an Englishman called Francis Crick.

BUILDING BLOCKS

Although our bodies look solid, they are actually made up of more than 100 trillion tiny cells. At the center of each cell is something called DNA. This substance includes all the information needed for us to live, reproduce, and pass on our characteristics to our children.

DNA contains thousands of pairs of genes. Each gene includes a specific piece of information about us, such as our hair or eye color. Every single person's DNA is slightly different. It forms the code that defines who we are.

THE HUMAN GENOME PROJECT

The object of the Human Genome Project was to look closely at human DNA in order to find every different gene. By 2000, when the project was completed, scientists had worked out that each strand of human DNA includes some 23,000 genes (the exact same number as found in mice). Each one of these genes is responsible for a different piece of information about the human body and how it works.

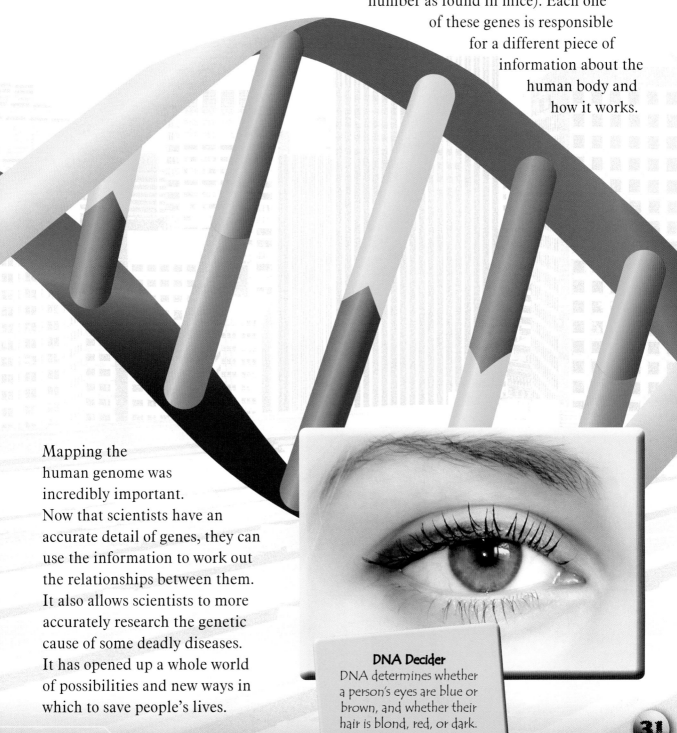

Mapping the human genome was incredibly important. Now that scientists have an accurate detail of genes, they can use the information to work out the relationships between them. It also allows scientists to more accurately research the genetic cause of some deadly diseases. It has opened up a whole world of possibilities and new ways in which to save people's lives.

DNA Decider
DNA determines whether a person's eyes are blue or brown, and whether their hair is blond, red, or dark.

Genetic Modification

Many dangerous diseases are genetic. This means that they develop because of damaged, defective genes. For those suffering from genetic diseases and conditions, understanding the way genes work offers hope for future treatments and even a potential cure.

INHERITED DISEASES

Genetic diseases are particularly devastating because they are passed down through families. If a parent has a genetic illness, it is possible that the child will suffer from the same thing. Sometimes, people can be lucky and are not affected by the disease. However, their children might suffer from the illness instead.

The Gene Lottery
Genetically inherited diseases can skip a generation, passing from one person but appearing in their child.

NO CURE

In the past, genetic disease have simply been incurable. For those suffering from crippling illnesses such as cystic fibrosis (a disease of the lungs), Huntington's disease (a disease that gets worse as the sufferer gets older), and Alport syndrome (a disease that results in kidney failure), there is little hope of recovery.

EARLY DAYS

Around the world, many scientists are currently working on research that could end the problem of genetic diseases for good. Scientists are looking at two different methods to cure genetic diseases. The first is gene adaptation. This means altering the make-up of someone's DNA so that the genes naturally adapt and become healthy ones instead.

The second method involves replacing the damaged cells that cause these diseases to develop with new cells containing healthy genes. Both methods are in their early stages, and as yet scientists have had little success.

Gene Control
If scientists master gene adaptation, in the future no babies will be born with genetic diseases.

Winning or Losing?

It's only been 12 years since the human genome was mapped out. Since then, doctors have had some success in using healthy stem cells to repair damaged body parts, but they have had little success in treating genetic disorders. Human genes are incredibly complicated, and it could take years to develop successful cures.

33

Fighting Cancer

Every year, more than 7 million people around the world are told that they have cancer. According to research, more than 13 percent of all deaths worldwide are because of cancer. It is for this reason that finding successful treatments is a huge scientific priority worldwide.

HOW CANCER WORKS

Cancer is a term used for diseases in which abnormal cells divide without control. To begin with, cancerous cells may affect just a small part of the body. They can divide and form a tumor—a cluster of infected cells. If the tumor isn't removed and the cancerous cells killed quickly, the disease may spread farther and eventually cause death.

Treating Cancer
Leukemia is a form of cancer that affects children and some adults. The treatment is chemotherapy, which results in loss of hair.

LOOKING FOR CURES

Scientists have been searching for a cure for cancer for many years. Some successful treatments have been developed, such as chemotherapy and radiation therapy. The best chance of curing the cancer is if the disease is diagnosed at an early stage. The type of cancer also affects a person's chance of survival because some types of cancer respond much better to treatment than others.

SO MANY CANCERS

One of the biggest difficulties facing cancer research scientists is the huge number of different forms of the disease. There are well over 200 different types of cancer and each affects the body in a different way.

In the Ring

In 1896, American doctor Emil Grubbe built an X-ray machine. He used it to give the first ever radiation therapy treatment to a woman with breast cancer. It was unsuccessful, but his idea stuck and was eventually developed into a safe and successful procedure.

FINDING CURES

Many billions of dollars are spent each year on cancer research. This money enables scientists to carefully study different areas and work on different theories. Some scientists concentrate on investigating the relationship between our genes and the disease. Others try to develop new, more effective drugs that help the body destroy any cancerous cells.

Looking for Cancer

Cancer growths inside the body can be detected using high-tech MRI scanners.

Chapter Four: The Future

Despite all of science's many great successes in fighting disease, there are still many illnesses and conditions for which there are no cures. It is these that scientists will be concentrating on in the future.

Race for a Cure
Finding a cure for the deadly HIV virus (right) is one of the most pressing issues facing scientists.

HUMAN BRAIN

One of the parts of the human body that we know little about is the brain. Much research is being done to try and work out what causes brain diseases and how we can treat and cure them.

Millions of people suffer from very destructive diseases of the brain, from depression and schizophrenia to Alzheimer's and Parkinson's disease. At this time, there are no cures for these diseases, just treatments that can make people's lives a little better.

Some scientists think that the key to curing brain diseases may lie in our genes, but this is an area we know little about. In the years to come, scientists will be working hard to find the answers.

CURING HIV

Scientists in laboratories around the world are desperately searching for a cure to HIV/AIDS. At present, there are thought to be around 34 million people in the world infected with HIV. Around 2 million people die each year because of the virus. One of the great hopes is that scientists will one day be able to develop a vaccine that protects against HIV. Since scientists have been working on one for 30 years without success, it could be years before a cure is found.

Breaking Through

In April 2012, scientists at UCLA in Los Angeles happily announced the successful trial of a potential cure for HIV. The treatment involves injecting special blood cells that are designed to hunt down and kill body cells infected with HIV. The treatment has proved successful on mice, but has yet to be tested on humans.

Dealing with Mental Illness
Diseases such as depression can leave the victim unable to cope with life.

Clone Zone

Mapping the human genome has brought the possibility of cloning humans closer. Cloning means creating an identical copy. While this is not yet possible, scientists are beginning to discover ways of cloning particular body parts, such as skin cells and the soft tissue inside organs such as the heart and lungs.

Recreating Cells
It is now possible for scientists to make exact copies of human body cells in a laboratory.

HOW IT WORKS

The idea behind cloning is simple. All of the cells in a person's body include the same bundle of genes that makes up DNA. If a scientist copied a person's DNA exactly and put it into an embryo, he or she could, in theory, create an exact copy of that person.

No scientist has done this successfully yet, and it is something that very few people would actually like to see. Many people think that tampering with life in this way is against nature. Scientists have successfully cloned animals such as sheep and pigs, but most have lived short lives.

Right or Wrong?
Is it right or wrong to be able to clone humans? This is one of the most talked-about subjects of our age.

GENE THERAPY

One area where cloning is helping people is therapeutic cloning. This means cloning important cells, called stem cells, to help repair damaged parts of the body. These types of procedures are often called stem cell treatments, and they hold the key to the cure for many different diseases.

Bone marrow transplantation is an example of stem cell treatment. In this process, healthy stem cells are placed inside the bones of cancer patients. The stem cells grow into healthy new bone marrow. In experiments, scientists have also successfully inserted cloned body cells into damaged hearts and grown new skin cells for people injured in fires.

Breaking Through

On November 25, 2003, a woman in Korea managed to stand on her own and walk without assistance for the first time in 19 years. This was achieved after scientists injected healthy adult stem cells into the damaged part of the woman's back.

Prevention Over Cure

When scientists announced that they had mapped the human genome, it allowed researchers to begin unlocking the secrets of genetic diseases. Now, scientists are using this knowledge to try to prevent dangerous genetic diseases from taking hold.

Affected in Old Age
Genetic diseases such as Alzheimer's affect the brain in old age, meaning people struggle to think and care for themselves.

MUTATIONS

People with genetic diseases have a missing, defective, or mutated gene somewhere in their DNA. Scientists believe that we need to work out which genes cause certain diseases or conditions. It might then be possible to remove or replace those genes and stop these diseases from taking hold.

OLD AGE AND DISEASE

Some of the most damaging diseases are caused by genetic mutations, particularly those usually associated with old age. Many genetic diseases affect older people. Scientists think there is a link between certain genes and the development of brain diseases such as Alzheimer's and Parkinson's in old age. Both of these diseases cause people to lose control of their mind and body over a period of time.

EARLY CURE

If the key to curing these diseases is to prevent them by replacing genes early in life, it will change the world we live in. Children would have their DNA tested and have any defective genes "switched off" or replaced. They could then live indefinitely, maintaining near perfect health for well over 100 years. It's currently just an idea, but it may one day become reality.

Cruel Disease
Brain disease can dramatically reduce the life quality of not only the sufferer, but also their caretakers.

Winning or Losing?
The science of gene therapy is only in its early stages, and as yet there have been few breakthroughs. However, scientists are constantly finding new links between genes and certain diseases. It is only a matter of time before successful ways of switching off disease-causing genes are found.

The Fight Continues: Is Science Winning?

Science has helped us make great progress in battling disease and illness. We now live longer, healthier lives. We know more about the body and how it works than ever before, but there is still much that we don't know. Can scientists continue to create cures and develop technology that will save lives in the future?

NEVER-ENDING TASK

Scientists face a difficult challenge in fighting disease. There will always be new diseases that take us by surprise, new infections that sweep the world, and new versions of deadly diseases that put medicine back by many years.

Scientists also face a constant battle with human nature. We often eat the wrong foods, pollute our lungs by smoking, take dangerous drugs, or lead generally unhealthy lives. Scientists can advise us not to do these things, but they can't stop us. All they can do is come up with cures for the diseases caused by these negative lifestyle choices.

Doctors' Warnings
Despite warnings from doctors, many people continue unhealthy activities, such as smoking, drinking, and taking drugs.

CHALLENGES AHEAD

Finding cures for dangerous infections and genetic disorders are still the biggest challenges facing scientists. These illnesses are very complex, so it could be another 20 or more years before effective treatments are found. There is also a real possibility that a deadly new strain of super-strength flu could emerge at any time.

The battle against all deadly disease will probably never be won, but scientists will find a cure for many. Thanks to the amazing scientific advances of both the past and the present, many people can now live longer and healthier lives.

Doing the Right Thing
Thanks to science, we now know how to care for our bodies and make healthy lifestyle choices.

Breaking Through

In November 2011, scientists at the University of San Diego in the United States announced that they had developed a revolutionary wonder drug that may cure cancer in the future. The drug, named KG5, works by attacking and destroying cancer tumors. The drug could be on sale by 2016.

The Disease Story

1030
Avicenna writes the first medical textbooks, *The Book of Healing* and *The Canon of Medicine*.

1796
English doctor Edward Jenner invents the first successful smallpox vaccine.

1816
Rene Laennec invents the stethoscope, which allows doctors to listen to the heartbeats of their patients for the first time.

1846
First "painless" operation performed using new drugs called anesthetics, to numb the pain.

1870
Scientists Louis Pasteur and Robert Koch offer the theory that most diseases are caused by tiny germs.

1946
Alfred G. Gilman and Louis S. Goodman introduce chemotherapy as a possible cure for cancer.

1953
Dr. John Heysham Gibbon builds the first ever heart-lung machine with General Motors and uses it while operating on a woman in Detroit.

1953
The first ultrasound sonograph machine is built, allowing doctors to check on the health of babies before they are born.

1953
James D. Watson and Francis Crick discover the structure of human DNA.

1954
Surgeon Joseph Murray performs the first ever kidney transplant operation.

1971
Two revolutionary new types of scanners, MRI and CT/CAT, are invented and allow doctors to see inside the human body without surgery.

1895
Wilhelm Conrad Rontgen discovers that radiation X-rays can be used to look inside the human body.

1910
Swedish doctor Hans Christian Jacobaeus performs the first ever keyhole surgery operation.

1928
Alexander Fleming discovers penicillin.

1931
Ernst Ruska and Max Knoll build the first electron microscope.

1943
Willem J. Koff builds the first ever kidney dialysis machine.

1978
A researcher in Birmingham, England, becomes the last person to die of smallpox.

1996
First drugs to treat HIV/AIDS are launched.

1998
James Thomson perfects the first successful stem cell therapy treatment.

2000
President Bill Clinton and Prime Minister Tony Blair announce the mapping of the human genome.

2001
Jacques Marescaux performs the first keyhole surgery operation using a tiny camera.

2003
SARS virus discovered. First vaccine produced within months.

2010
Surgeon Laurent Lantieri performs the first full face transplant.

Glossary

blueprint a plan of action

cells tiny "building blocks" that make up all living things

defective something that doesn't work properly

dialysis the process by which the kidneys clean our blood. A dialysis machine is used to do this job when someone's kidneys stop working.

DNA the bundle of genes at the center of every human body cell that carries vital information about us

donor someone who gives something to somebody else free of charge

embryo an unborn baby at a very early point in pregnancy

epidemic an outbreak of a disease that spreads rapidly over a large area

gene therapy the process of curing disease by altering genes that do not work correctly, or contain information that leads to the development of an illness

genes the information contained in our DNA

genetic diseases diseases that are passed down from parents to their children in their genes

human genome all of the genetic information in a person

incubator a machine that helps premature babies to breathe and which keeps them warm

infection a disease that enters the body from an outside source

mutate something that changes into something else

nervous system the body's system of nerves, tissues, and muscles that respond to a stimulus

pacemaker a small device that is inserted into the body during surgery to help a person's heart to perform normally

pandemic a disease epidemic that has spread to other parts of the world

paralyzed losing the use of parts of your body due to an accident or illness

premature born too soon. Premature babies are born before they have had time to fully develop within the uterus.

prosthetic limbs legs or arms that are made from man-made materials and created for people who have lost a limb

radiation the process by which energy travels through objects

resistant unaffected

stem cell treatment a treatment that involves replacing diseased body cells with healthy ones

tropical disease a disease that occurs in areas of the world found near the equator. The equator is an imaginary line around the middle of the planet.

vaccine a medicine designed to protect the body against a specific disease or group of diseases

white blood cells body cells that travel around the body in blood and protect us against disease

World Health Organization an international charity dedicated to issues surrounding the health of people around the world

For More Information

BOOKS

Hindley, Judy, and C.J. Rawson. *How Your Body Works*.
London, UK: Usborne Books, 1995.

Koellhoffe, Tara. *Science News for Kids: Health and Medicine*.
New York, NY: Chelsea House Publishers, 2006.

VanGorp, Lynn. *Genetics*. Mankato, MN: Compass Point, 2009.

WEBSITES

You can find lots of information about staying
healthy, how the body works, and illnesses at:
kidshealth.org/kid

Click the links on the left to explore the human body at:
www.kidsbiology.com/human_biology/index.php

Browse the links on the Science News for Kids website
for fascinating articles on human health at:
www.sciencenewsforkids.org/category/health

Publisher's note to educators and parents: Our editors have carefully reviewed these
websites to ensure that they are suitable for students. Many websites change frequently,
however, and we cannot guarantee that a site's future contents will continue to meet
our high standards of quality and educational value. Be advised that students should
be closely supervised whenever they access the Internet.

Index